WHEN DEATH
COMES KNOCKING

A woman's night of unspeakable horror and her decade long search for justice. A testimony to her faith in God and the significance of forensic science.

By

B. Kaye Robinson

with Tony E. Windsor

Featured on an episode of the
Forensic Files® television series

Foreword by Paul Dowling,
Producer and Creator of
Forensic Files®

Copyright © 2011 Robinson/Windsor
Kayton Publishing
All rights reserved.
ISBN-13:978-0615462714

Dedicated to those who know the power of love
and use it in service to others.

T. Windsor

Foreword

If you were to spend an entire summer watching nothing but Forensic Files television shows, 5 days a week, 8 hours a day, you still wouldn't see every episode. We've produced hundreds and hundreds of them in the fifteen years the series has been in production. It's safe to say I know a good true crime story when I see one. Our episode about Kaye Robinson's case is one of the best we've ever produced. Why? Because her story challenges many of our long held beliefs about crime scene investigations and our criminal justice system.

In the century of science, most of us think that forensic science is absolute, that it always identifies the guilty. We also give enormous weight to circumstantial evidence. We hear a gunshot, we run outside, we see a man holding a gun, standing over a dead body. We conclude the man holding the gun just killed the dead man. Are we right? Maybe not. When a victim walks into the courtroom, puts her hand on the bible, swears to tell the truth, points to the person at the defense table and says "That's the man who raped and stabbed me," we believe her. Will the jury really vote "not guilty" after that? And what about people who confess? "I'm guilty, your honor. I killed my girlfriend." Open and shut case, right? That happened once in Nevada but the girlfriend returned several days later, refreshed from a short vacation. Good thing executions weren't done the same day as convictions. Kaye Robinson's case incorporates all this and more!

Tony Windsor, who played an important role in our Forensic Files episode, does a masterful job, taking the reader through the many twists and turns of a story that simply defies logic. As I've said thousands of times, if you wrote these stories as novels, readers wouldn't believe them. But you don't have to suspend disbelief when you read about actual crime. That's the best part. The worst part is that the victims are real people, whose wounds never really heal. Tony Windsor knows that, too, which is why he's the perfect author for Kaye's story.

Paul Dowling
Executive Producer & Creator
Forensic Files® television series

Preface

Dateline: Laurel - September, 1995

The sour taste that violence leaves in your soul takes on an even more caustic flavor when it affects someone you know. We all find ourselves shaking our heads in empathy when we read the headlines telling about someone who has been hurt or killed by senseless acts of aggression.

But the horror of violence becomes totally real only when we are able to attach a familiar face to the hapless victim. So it is that while I am writing this column I see in my mind the face of a dear friend who is the victim of such a senseless and despicable act of violence.

Last week's attack of a Laurel woman at her mobile home leaves me feeling a great deal of shock, sadness and bitterness. The victim of this attack is a friend of mine. She is a friend to many people in this area. Those who know her know her to be kind, compassionate and above all else, a loving and dedicated mother.

Here is a woman who as a single mother has spent years raising her son and committing herself to being a good mother, daughter, sister and friend. She never turns a deaf ear to someone who may be having a problem or just wants to talk or ask for some advice. It is often that you would find her playing parent and friend to a houseful of local children. These kids know her and respect her. They respect her because she has proven herself to be someone who cares about them.

My heart breaks whenever I think of this hard-working mother having to face the outrageous acts of repulsive evil that were unleashed on her in the early morning hours of Sept. 19. In the privacy of her home her castle - someone broke in and viciously attacked her. For no reason this woman was brutally assaulted.

Her commitment to motherhood, her dedication to family, her compassion for friends and her loyal work ethic;

none of this mattered. The heartless, cowardly acts of a brutal animal took its toll on another helpless victim.

Since this attack, communities have been outraged and continue to ask why. Why would someone do this to another human being? Why did this happen to a woman who works so hard to be a good person? There have always been evil people who have preyed on our society. However, it seems that the arrogance of these evil people has become overwhelming.

As a child I remember my parents leaving the windows and doors open during the heat of the summer. Long walks late at night were commonplace. No more. There seems to be no safe haven, including our homes, that protects us from the perpetrators of violence.

Perhaps we only need look at the decay of the moral fibers that make up the fabric of our society. Slowly we have become in many ways not unlike the animals that we are supposed to be superior to. The difference is that most animals attack as a means of protection and survival.

We are becoming a nation of people who have placed little value on human life. There are those in our society who, because of dependence on drugs, the desire for money and'. power, or other selfish, irrational reasons, will viciously turn on' those of our own species.

This is fortunately the attitude of a minority of people. But, in order' to counteract the actions of this brutal minority, we as the majority of caring human beings must become even more involved in helping to protect one another.

We must return to the days, when the community as a whole helped to raise its children and citizens watched each others homes and looked out for their neighbor's property as if it were their own. These are ways to help assure that the horrors of last week are not repeated.

A beautiful, caring mother lies in the hospital, the undeserving victim of violence. Out of respect to her and the millions of others who have fallen prey to this barbaric tyranny, we must begin to come together and help restore a moral character to our society. Less than this leaves these victims nothing more than statistics.

Column by Tony E. Windsor published in the September 27, 1995 issue of the Seaford Leader/State Register newspaper, Seaford, Delaware

Introduction

Life to me has always been a series of events, none of which outside of the birth of my son, have I considered extraordinary. I think I have always enjoyed having the normality of my life serving as a definition of my lifestyle. I have a wonderful family, a son who I adore, a mother who has always been more like a best friend to me and two sisters with whom I have been very close. I love having an ordinary life. I guess my "ordinary life" always made me feel somewhat comfortable and secure. As a single mother to a young son, I always had my fair share of day-to-day challenges, including the bills, keeping the house and balancing my role as a Mom with that of being a working woman. But, in all, I was always fine with that life.

It seems I met each day with little proactive consideration. I did not rely on any type of faith to guide me. The spiritual side of my life was always relegated to a more private, low-profile component of my daily routine. I have always believed in God, but generally kept my faith stored in the inner most places of my soul. I was never comfortable "preaching" to friends about salvation or putting myself in a position which might result in surrendering my own sense of confidence. I was the consummate "strong, independent woman," and I found a great source of pride in that.

As we have learned over the years from Biblical principal, "pride comes before the fall." I do not necessarily believe the turn of events that drew me closer to God were the result of my being too prideful or that I thought myself not needing of a more intimate walk with The Father. I truly believe as I faced the piercing, steel-cold eyes of evil and felt the hot breath of death, I was simply allowed to feel in the midst of this terror, that He was present and would not let the forces of Hell prevail.

Before I open the door to the past and allow myself to re-visit the horror that forced its way into my "ordinary life," I want to acknowledge that my very ability to do so comes through the grace and protecting love of God, who allowed me to survive it. It is my sincere desire to share my story as a source of inspiration and a testimony of how remarkable God's love is and how His grace is truly sufficient in all things.

Brenda Kaye Robinson

Our Father who art in Heaven; Hallowed be thy name; Thy Kingdom come; Thy will be done; On earth as it is in Heaven; Give us this day our daily bread and forgive us our trespasses as we forgive those who trespass against us. Lead us not into temptation, but deliver us from evil, for thou is the Kingdom, the Power and the Glory forever...Amen.
Matthew 6:9-13 NIV

Chapter 1

I had lost the ability to breathe. I was struggling to find my breath as it seemed fear had literally consumed me and left my lungs void of air. I was running through the living room of what I always believed was a safe haven – my home. Stumbling past tables and lamps I was not sure where I was going as time seemed to stand still and I felt as though I was running in slow motion. All I could manage to force into my frantic mind was that I was facing death, or worse, and my

11-year-old son was helplessly sleeping in the nearby bedroom.

Suddenly, I realized no matter what happened to me, I had to keep this animal away from my child. It was not about being a "hero;" it is an instinct that God allows us to possess – an intrinsic desire to protect our children. But, just as quickly as this thought had come, so did the horrific realization that I was being gripped tightly in the clutches of what I would soon find to be worse than any monster I could have imagined occupying the pits of Hell. He was a man, but at that moment he was a killer and rapist; a hunter and I was his prey.

Alone, with no one to hear me scream, except my son. And if I did scream, I risked waking my son, Nathan, and causing him to unknowingly walk out into the living room and face a fate similar to mine. "No, I must find a way not to scream," I thought. "I must find a way to keep this monster away from my son."

It was no longer my decision and instead my captor was quickly, and without warning, in charge. In charge of not only my movements, but my thoughts and most terrifyingly, the decision as to whether I would live or die and whether I would suffer while he contemplated the latter.

Welcome to Americana…..

I have spent my life living in a part of the country that I always felt could be depicted in a Normal Rockwell painting. It has a rural landscape and only in recent years have we gotten some of the major retail box stores like Wal-Mart and Big Lots.

The Seaford and Laurel areas of Sussex County Delaware, have traditionally been farming regions. Seaford, of course, also had a boom in the mid-1930s when the DuPont Company invented nylon and built a manufacturing plant there which at one time employed as many as 2,000 people. Sadly, or fortunately, however one may view it, farming in Seaford and Laurel seems to be dwindling in the face of commercial and residential development.

I was born in this area and raised by my mother, Eva, along with two sisters, Lora and Chris. We all grew up, went to school here and married men who were also from right here in Americana. Unfortunately, unlike my sisters, my marriage did not last. Perhaps this was largely due to the fact that neither my husband nor I were much more than in our mid-teens when we unwisely tied the knot. That is one of the perils of youth; action without clear thought or planning.

But, as unfortunate and unwise as the marriage may have been, it produced my son, Nathan, and for that I thank God every day. It was not easy raising a child as a single mother, but I am sure parents of healthy marriages would say the same thing. I never expected parenting to be easy, but I never regretted a moment of it, not even during the "terrible twos," and the rebellious teen years. I always viewed being a mother as the greatest honor I could have ever received from God. All the challenges that come with it simply make it a "labor of love".

For the most part, I was successful in making a home for my son and I worked as an insurance agent for a major company. As an insurance agent, it has always been customary for me to help people pick out policies for their vehicles, property and of course to use as a resource to plan for their family at the time of their death. Whenever discussing insurance, especially house and property insurance, we deal with "what ifs."

"What if someone breaks into your home and steals your television, or your favorite sports collection. What if vandals break your windows or damage your outside property? You will do well to protect your valuables," I would often say.

As real as the threat of someone breaking into the home is, I don't think I ever recall talking about it with a customer and giving it more than a casual thought or considering it much more plausible than the warning that flashes across the movie screen with information about what to do in case of a fire.

However, as autumn crept across southern Delaware in 1996, leaving the trees beaming with the festive colors of orange and red and a crisp, fresh breeze in the air, I was oblivious to just how real the threat of someone breaking into your home can be – and how deadly. Within a short span of time, I would be thrust headlong into a nightmare of brutality that would forever change my life.

An otherwise peaceful night.....

Morning seems to come earlier for me once autumn sets in. I love the season, but the days are so much shorter and I am sadly aware that the crisp, fresh mild temperatures of fall will soon transition into the crippling cold of winter. As I stood at the kitchen sink, drying the last of the dinner dishes, I pondered the busy schedule I would have the next day at work. Glancing at the living room clock, I saw it was almost 11 pm.; not a bad time to call it a night. I could get to bed, get a good night's sleep and be ready for another hectic day at the office.

My bedroom is on the far end of our mobile home and the entrance is from the kitchen. My son, Nathan's bedroom is on the opposite end of our home. So, before going to bed, I routinely check in on him then shut the lights off on my way back through the living room and kitchen, before making my way to my bed.

However, on this night Nathan had fallen asleep watching a movie in my bedroom, so rather than rouse him, I decided to let him sleep. It was late, so I decided to simply spend the night in his bedroom. It was a slightly smaller room and filled with all the things you would expect from an 11-year-old boy, including video games and the clothes he had worn that day, all lying around on the floor.

I lay quietly in his bed as the moon's light broke through the spaces between the venetian blinds of the bedroom window and shined a dim, but calming white light on the wall beside my bed. In a matter of minutes I was asleep.

"Boom, boom, boom"! The sound, seemingly louder than thunder, immediately ripped me from a deep sleep as it literally shook the walls of my home. Wiping the sleep from my eyes and attempting to bring a clear thought to mind, I rose up in the bed, gazing at the wall startled and somewhat frightened. The clock on the dresser near the bed read 12:45 am.

Trying to imagine who in the world could be beating on my door at such an ungodly hour, my first thought was to simply ignore this racket and go back to sleep. "Boom, boom, boom," once again the walls shook and it was clear this was not going to stop. As much as I dreaded the consideration, I was going to have to see who was at the door. I slowly rolled out of the comfortable bed and made my way in the dark across the living room to the small alcove where the kitchen door is located off to the right. It was just outside of my bedroom where Nathan continued sleeping. I got to the door and rose up on my tip-toes to peer through the glass window at the top of the door.

Immediately, my eyes fell upon the face of a grizzled, grungy-looking man, with glaring eyes that seemed to look through me. It was a site that caused me to jump back from fright and almost lose my balance. Rather than peer out the window and expose myself to this man, I spoke through the door.

"Who is it," I shouted toward the door? A voice answered back saying his car had broken down a few miles away and he needed to make a phone to call a friend for help. There was no question that I was not about to let this man into my home. I hollered back telling the man I would make a call for him.

'What is the number you need me to call, and who should I ask for," I asked the stranger. With little forethought, the man responded with a phone number and told me to ask for "Ben." I asked him what his name was. I could hear him pacing around in front of the steps leading to my kitchen door and the faint sound of his shoes kicking at the ground below him. "My name is Jack Wilson," he said.

I went to my phone in the living room and called the number. The phone began to ring and the voice of someone I had obviously awakened answered with a less than enthusiastic "Hello." I told the man on the other end of the phone that Jack had asked me to call and needed Ben to come to pick him up.

The man said there was no Ben at that residence and I must have dialed the wrong number. Apologizing, I said good bye and hung up the phone. I went back to the kitchen door and again yelled out to the stranger informing him that there was no one named Ben at the phone number he had given me. He became agitated and the kicking on the ground became harder and louder. "You must have dialed the wrong number," he exclaimed angrily. Considering that perhaps he was right, I asked him to repeat the number and I went back to make the call again.

I carefully dialed the phone number and I was greeted by the same agitated voice that I had just hung up from a few moments earlier. I apologized again. I told the man on the other end of the phone that there was a man at my door asking me to make this call and the man frightened me. I was hoping this would cause the man on the other end of the line to offer me some assurance, or perhaps give me some advice on what to do. I got neither.

He simply hung up the phone. Now becoming as much frustrated as scared, I made my way back to the kitchen door and informed "Jack Wilson" that the number was not correct and there was no "Ben" to be found. He became even angrier. "This is great," he proclaimed, using an expletive. He then kicked the ground one last time and walked off into the darkness and out of sight.

For I am convinced that neither death nor life, neither angels nor demons, neither the present nor the future, nor any powers, neither height nor depth, nor anything else in all creation, will be able to separate us from the love of God that is in Christ Jesus our Lord.
Romans 8:38,39 NIV

Chapter 2

When you are awaken during the wee hours of the morning it leaves you feeling as though you are the only person on earth who is awake. It is a peaceful, but lonely time; a time best dedicated to sleep. As I left the kitchen door and headed across the living room to check in on Nathan one last time before going back to bed, I possessed a very uneasy feeling. It lay like a stone in the pit of my stomach.

Who was this stranger beating on my door and why did his story about being stranded seem so suspicious, especially when he could not provide a phone number that seemed to support his story. My uneasy feeling led me to be convinced that there was no way I would return to anything close to sleep. The stranger was still out there and that alone gave me cause for concern.

I picked the phone back up and called the Delaware State Police. My call was answered by a police dispatcher. I explained the incident to her. I gave the dispatcher a description of the man and told her that he left me feeling as though something was simply not right. I would be comforted if a trooper could come by my mobile home park and make sure this man was truly gone. I made it clear that under no circumstances did I want the man to know that I had called the police. Given his agitated state when he left my yard, I did not want to have to worry about him having ill feelings toward me, especially when he knew where I lived.

The dispatcher assured me that a trooper would be coming by the mobile home park within the next few minutes and would attempt to locate the man, or at least make sure he was no longer in the area. This brought relief to me and suddenly I realized how tired I was. Although I felt somewhat more at ease, I decided I would finish the night out in my bedroom sleeping on the covers near my son. The night's events left me feeling the need to be near him, for both our sakes.

Waking to a nightmare....

Once again, an abrupt noise in the kitchen caused me to wake. This time I almost immediately recognized the sound as that of my door opening and slamming shut. I was not necessarily alarmed at this because I assumed it was my fiance, Andrew, who had a key to my home. He would traditionally stop by early mornings on his way to work to visit before I headed off for the office to start my work day. This was certainly a bit earlier than his normal visits, but it was hunting season and I guessed that he was coming by to have a cup of coffee before heading out to the nearby woods.

I once again crawled out the bed and rubbing the sleep from my eyes, I headed out of the bedroom. I glanced in the hallway mirror to make sure I was somewhat presentable before greeting Andrew. What I saw in the mirror's reflection immediately took my breath away and while standing almost paralyzed with fear I screamed in horror. It was the same stranger from earlier, this time crouched down beside a trash can in my kitchen holding a large butcher knife. He was waiting for me, like a demon, possessed by Satan. He was poised to strike and I had nowhere to hide.

Like an animal smelling his prey's fear, he was on me in seconds, grabbing me tightly as I struggled and begged. "Oh God, please don't hurt me, please," I cried in an almost whisper. "Shut up! I'm not going to hurt you," he screamed at me. I had no choice but to obey. I stopped struggling and gave in to his demands. "Who else is here," he asked. I was hesitant to reveal that my son was asleep in the next room. But, I feared should he find out that I lied to him, my son and I may both be in danger of serious harm. I told him Nathan was home, asleep in his bedroom.

"Let's go check on him" he said, shaking his head around with the eyes of a wild man. I once again begged him to not hurt my son. "I'm not going to hurt him, if he stays asleep. If he wakes up I will have to kill him though," he said in an eerie, matter-of-fact tone. He opened the door to my bedroom and turned to me and said, "Are you sure he is really asleep?" I told him I knew he was because I was familiar with how he breathed when he was sleeping.

He then reached up to turn on the bedroom light and I instinctively grabbed his hand. "Please don't turn on the light, you will wake him up," I pleaded, tears streaming down my face. Again, he asked me, "Are you sure he is asleep?" Again I told him that I knew when my son was really asleep and there was no question he was asleep. Little did I know that Nathan was not actually asleep. I learned later that he was lying there, pretending to sleep totally helpless as to what to do.

Turning toward me and gazing at me with the eyes of a maniac, the man once again warned me, "If he stays asleep he will be fine. But, if he wakes up I will kill him." He then reached to close the door, but a broken hinge made the job awkward and clumsy. He pushed on the door, trying to force it shut. He was making so much noise I just knew Nathan would be awaken and risk having the stranger fulfill his threat of killing him right in front of my eyes. The thought sent chills through my body and though paralyzed with fear, I attempted to calmly recommend how to get the door to shut.

I told him that the hinge on the door was broken and he would have to slightly lift the door to allow it to close more easily. Surprisingly, he did just what I told him and after shutting the door, walked us away from my son's bedroom and into the living room.

Pulling me by the arm, he led me to the living room couch and ordered me to sit. He kept looking around the room as if he was looking for something in particular; but his eyes were so wild, as if he were about to go totally crazy.

"Do you have any money or drugs," he asked? I told him that I only had seven dollars and some prescription pain medicine left over from a recent surgery. "Where's the money," he demanded? I was so scared that it was difficult for me to concentrate. I could not remember where I had put the money. I suddenly remembered that the money was in my cigarette case on the kitchen table.

I got up to retrieve the cigarette case and he immediately grabbed me and thrust me back down on the couch. "No! Wait, wait! I will do that," he said violently. He grabbed the cigarette case and asked where the money was kept. I explained it was in the zippered front compartment of the case. From the point on he began asking me a series of questions as if he was drilling me to see if I would lie to him, as if he actually knew the answer to each question.

"You don't mind if I smoke your cigarettes do you," he asked as he lit one. "I didn't think you would mind," he said in a taunting manner. "Are you expecting any company," he asked, continuing the line of questioning. I told him that I was not expecting anyone. He then asked what time I went to work. "Eight o'clock," I responded. "What time does your son have to get up for school," he asked?

I told him that Nathan usually got up around 6:30 am.. One after another the questions kept coming. If I were not sitting with a madman, it would have been no more different than a casual conversation with a new acquaintance. But, this was not an acquaintance. This was a man who seemed ready to explode; a man who left me unsure of when the moment would come when he tired of the casual banter and decided to murder me and my son.

As he smoked his cigarette, my cigarette actually, I continued to plead with him to not hurt me or my child. I offered to give him anything he wanted in the house if he would just leave and not harm us. This was the most alone, the most vulnerable, I have ever felt. Time was no longer an element; it had long ago stopped. I was frozen in a moment of extreme fear and uncertainty. I could not fathom at that moment which was worse, the fact that I could be facing death, or by what means that death would come.

I watched him sitting there, smoking the cigarette with an air of obnoxious arrogance that made me disgusted. But, he was in control and he knew it. He had me afraid and uncertain, two emotions that were working in his favor, and against me. I glanced around at the inside of the home that had always been my place of security; my haven from harm. It was now my prison, and soon to become my torture chamber.

Once again he started asking about money and if I had more somewhere in the house. I explained that I was a single mother and simply did not have much money. "Don't play that innocent victim s—t with me," he said in an agitated manner. I assured him that I was not trying to deceive him and I was being completely honest with him.

He asked about the whereabouts of my purse. I was so confused by this point I felt like telling him that I could not remember where anything was and if he wanted it he could look for it himself. However, I had the presence of mind to realize that that would be a very foolish thing to say, given my predicament.

I found the purse and he grabbed it from my hand. He made me sit on the bed in my bedroom while he rifled through my purse, He pulled out my checkbook and I immediately told him to take the checks if he wanted them. He looked over to a desk and saw some money lying out in the open. "Whose money is that?" he asked, as if it really mattered.

I explained that my son had been cutting grass and raking leaves earlier in the day and had earned the money. His next comment took me by surprise. "I can't take that. It wouldn't be right," he said in what appeared to be a sincere tone. I found it hard to believe, but I was ready to let him have the money. I would replace it, anything to get this animal out of my house and away from me and my son.

Suddenly, from out of nowhere, he changed the direction of the conversation and asked me where I kept a clock. It took me a second or so to rearrange my thoughts and focus on something other than his previous search for money. I explained that I had no clocks, but did have a watch. For some reason this seemed to anger him. He questioned why I had no clocks on my walls. I tried to explain that there is a clock on the coffee pot in the kitchen and one on the VCR below my television in the living room;

other than those, I have a watch. He made a sarcastic remark and said, "Where is it? Let's go get it."

I thought I had left it in the living room and sure enough, it was lying on the bar that separates that room from my small kitchen, where this nightmare had started. I walked toward the watch on the bar and rather than move with me as I expected, he drifted off to the kitchen. He reached for a glass and opened the refrigerator. I cannot be sure what he took out, but he poured it in the glass and drank. He then sat the empty glass back on the table.

He turned toward me, but as if struck with a sudden burst of reality, he immediately turned back around and reached down and picked up the glass and began wiping it off with his shirt sleeve. "Oops! Forgot the fingerprints," he said looking at me with an expression of arrogance that suggested he felt quite superior in his knowledge of covering his criminal tracks.

He wiped the glass extensively and then in a completely contradictory action, used his other hand to set the glass back on the table, making his previous efforts for naught.

This completely amazed me. He took the time to wipe fingerprints off the glass just to put fingerprints from his other hand all over the glass.

Unfortunately, it was also obvious to me that if he took the time to recognize the need to wipe away evidence linking him to being in my home, there was a good chance his continued presence could very well result in an even worse outcome. He glared at me and began to explain his actions. "I can't leave any evidence," he said in a tone that was demonstrative of the same degree of arrogance. "I know that when I leave the first thing you are going to do is call the cops."

Suddenly, for the first time since this madman had invaded my home, I heard something that left me with a glimmer of hope. He uttered the word "leave." He actually made a reference to leaving my home. I had to convince him that I would never call the police; all I wanted was for him to leave without hurting me or my son. I began to assure him that I would not call the police. I told him he could have anything in my home he wanted, if he would just leave and not hurt us. My pleas fell on deaf ears. He was not moved by my passion and instead became agitated and cold. "I can have anything I want anyway, so shut the f—k up," he said taking me by the arm.

Still clenching the knife in one hand he led me with the other. We arrived at my son's bedroom door and my heart and thoughts began to race. I could not let him get me through that door. I could only wrap my mind around one explanation for why he would suddenly want to force me into the bedroom and that thought seemed to leave me even more horrified than my earlier thoughts of his killing me.

For momentary, light affliction is producing for us an eternal weight of glory far beyond all comparison, while we look not at the things which are seen, but at the things which are not seen; for the things which are seen are temporal, but the things which are not seen are eternal.
2 Corinthians 4:17,18 NASB

Chapter 3

Almost as in a dream, I could hear the muffled sound of a car's motor not 10-feet away from my front door steps. As it passed by my house I suddenly realized that life was normal out there. Within 50-yards on either side of my home there were people sleeping comfortably in their bedrooms, others perhaps watching a late night movie. No one was aware that my home had been transformed into a stark, cold, inhumane house of horror.

I felt the filthy fingers of the stranger attempt to push me into the bedroom. Much like someone drowning, I clenched the door frame and frantically tried to keep my body outside in the living room. I fought with every ounce of energy I could muster. He grabbed my hand and twisted my fingers away from the door frame. But, almost instinctively, I would push him away and grab the door ledge with my other hand. I believed with every fiber of my being that if he got me in that bedroom I would never come out alive.

He became increasingly angry as I fought him off. He warned me during our struggle that he was not alone. Further more, he said I should be grateful that it was him who had broken into my home rather than his colleague. "There is someone out there who is meaner than me," he said, catching his breath as he attempted to break the hold I had on the door frame. "You should be glad I came in here and not him,' he said, suddenly leaning back and thrusting the knife in my face. At this point, I could not consider whether or not he was telling the truth about there being someone else outside my home. At this very moment I could only deal with the man who was in my home and who I felt was about to rape me.

He waived the knife around my face and sides of my head, taunting me as if each time I should be prepared for the next thrust to make contact. Almost without thinking, I grabbed the top portion of the knife's blade and we began struggling with the weapon. The harder I tried to force the blade out of his hand, the more force he exerted. It was obvious to me I did not have the power it would take to wrestle the knife out of his grip.

It was then that I decided to try and break off the blade of the knife to make it a little less threatening. I frantically grabbed at the knife as he maneuvered it through the air. I knew I was taking a massive chance, but I felt if I could find a way to somehow break off the blade of the knife, I would be in less immediate danger. Somehow I managed to grab the knife blade and a vicious tug of war ensued between this monster and me.

I pushed against the blade as he yanked the knife erratically, trying to gain back his full control. Suddenly, I felt the blade snap and I was holding it in my hand. I was caught off guard because I was not prepared for the blade to break so quickly. Once I realized what had happened I threw the blade into my son's bedroom, behind his bed. Though the knife's blade was broken the man continued to lunge at me with what was now nothing more than a wooden handle.

He suddenly realized his weapon was now useless and noticed that he had been cut in the struggle and was bleeding. "Ain't that some s—t. I brought the knife and I'm the one who got cut," he said snickering under his breath. Sensing an opportunity, I bolted past him and raced through the living room, screaming for Nathan to wake up and get out of the house. I grabbed the telephone and started dialing. Before I could even get the first number dialed for 911, he was yanking the phone from my hands and slamming it to the floor.

He demanded I stop fighting him and "shut up." He called me a "bitch," and ordered me to go to in the bedroom. As he grabbed my arm I resisted and pulled in the opposite direction. I was determined to keep him from getting me into the bedroom, but he dragged me kicking and screaming to the bedroom door. I managed to wrap my leg around the door ledge and pushed my shoulder against him, knocking him against the wall. I pushed my shoulder into his chest and grabbed his wrists, creating a wedge that I knew I could not withstand for very long.

Again I yelled to my son, hoping he would wake up and while I was wrestling with this barbarian, he could get outside and go for help. With my son out of the house and safe I would have no concern about using whatever means to fight for my life. Still my pleas did not arouse my sleeping son.

As the stranger fought to regain his control, he one again warned me that he was not alone. "There's somebody else outside and if you don't shut the hell up we will kill your son," he said. Spit flew from his mouth as he angrily fought against me and continued his threats. Was he telling the truth? Was there really another madman outside my house prepared to come inside to help finish what this first maniac had started? It was too big a risk for me to take.

I could barely hold off one man, two would surely leave me completely defenseless. I immediately began apologizing for my actions. "Please, I'm sorry. I am just so scared you are going to hurt us," I pleaded. Unaffected by my pleas he once again took control of the situation. "If you don't shut up and stop fighting me I am going to show you what I am going to do," he shouted at me. He then went into my son's room; I suspected to retrieve the blade of the knife. Once again I began pleading.

"Please don't get the blade. If you don't get the blade I know you won't hurt us," I said. He made it clear that it was necessary for him to find the knife. "I can't leave any evidence for the cops to find," he muttered. Despite my repeated promise to not involve the police, he continued his quest. "Sure you won't call the cops. You must think I am an idiot. I know what you are going to do the minute I leave here," he ranted. As he fought to regain his composure and catch his breath from our struggle, he decided we would go and check on my son. "If you shut up and don't fight me, I won't kill him," he threatened. He led me back to my bedroom where I was thankful my son still lay safe. I wondered how Nathan had managed to remain asleep during the entire struggle and all the yelling. Now I realize that he was not asleep, but lying there not knowing whether to jump up and try to run out the backdoor, or run to my aid and fight off this crazed man. Either option left the potential for risking both our lives. I am happy that he simply lay there silently absorbing the horrible sounds of my attack.

I sought to find any small sign that God was somehow present in the midst of this hell; thinking my son was sleeping soundly and oblivious to the nightmare was evidence to me of the grace of God. The stranger was satisfied that Nathan was asleep and we left the room.

Heading across the living room floor toward my son's bedroom my mind was frenzied as I searched to think of a plan of action that could somehow allow Nathan to escape the house. If I just knew my son was out of the house and safe, I would use anything within my grasp to fight this monster. In the bedroom I was pushed to the bed and ordered to keep my mouth shut and stay on the bed. The man then reached for one of my cigarettes, hung it loosely in his mouth and lit it. "Marlboro Light; you're a real cowgirl. Yea you are," he said smiling with a sinister grin. Once again he told me to "shut up." He then told me he needed to look around for something to take from the house.

What did he mean? He could have the entire house if he wanted it. I could care less. Just do not hurt my son or me. Then it struck me like a fist in my stomach, knocking away any hope I had of an end to this nightmare. He was looking for something he could take so that when he leaves the house it will look like a robbery. Oh my God, he is planning to hurt us.

As he left the room and searched the living room and kitchen, I slowly rose from the bed. I cautiously went to the bedroom door and peeked out to see where he was. I could see him at the backdoor, leaning outside as if he were talking to someone outside the door. Now I was convinced he was not lying. There was someone else outside. Suddenly he turned and spied me standing at the door. He became enraged and headed back toward the bedroom. I was frantic. I immediately began apologizing and trying to explain that I was simply scared, again begging him to not hurt me. In the bedroom he ordered me to sit down and began telling me what was going to happen. "This is how it is going to be. You are going to shut your mouth and stop fighting me and you are going to let me tie you up. If not, I am going to kill your son. It is that simple." My heart stopped. I then made him promise me that he would not hurt my son. I was dealing with a mad man, but I still needed to hear him assure me that my son would not be hurt.

The decision I had to make was a choice between two horrors: continue to fight and risk him keeping his promise to kill my son, or allow him to tie me up and leave me completely helpless and under his absolute control. The only choice that seemed to give my son a chance was to be tied up. I said a silent prayer and told him I would concede to being tied up. Immediately he reached for the Super Nintendo® video game console that lay nearby. He cut the cord off and thrust it around my wrists. He began tying my wrists so quickly and tightly that my hands started to become numb before he finished. As I felt the restriction of my hands I suddenly began to second-guess my decision. I was now totally helpless to do anything if this monster decided to go back on his word and hurt my son.

He walked out of the room and I panicked. Was he heading to my son's room to hurt him? I could not take the chance, so I rolled off the bed and out the door. When I got to the living room I could see him fumbling through the dishes I had left in the kitchen sink. Suddenly he turned to see me standing in the living room.

"You can't do a damn thing I tell you, can you," he barked? I again explained that I was just scared he would hurt my son. "I said I wouldn't hurt your fu—ing son," he shouted. He then turned and opened a drawer on the kitchen sink and pulled out a wooden-handled steak knife. He also grabbed paper towels from the counter and headed back toward the bedroom. He motioned for me to move back into the bedroom and I once again sat helplessly on the bed, fearing what might be coming.

I begged him to please stop what he was doing. I told him he could have my car, or anything else he wanted if he would just stop this madness and leave now. I promised I would never speak to the police, or anyone else about what had happened. I just wanted him to leave so I could be assured no harm would come to me or my son. But, he had gone to far to stop; he was like a mad dog with the taste of blood in his mouth and he wanted more.

As he approached me I am sure it was clear to him that I was petrified, almost to the point of paralysis. Of course I was fearing what he was planning to do to me, but even more I feared what he might do to my son once he was finally finished with me. I was helpless to do anything; my son lay innocently sleeping just a few feet away and I was tied up and unable to keep him safe. Why did I let him tie me up? I blamed myself, but what choice did I have?

The cold steel of the knife pressed against the top of my left shoulder as he slipped the blade up under my nightshirt and quickly cut it loose. He then moved to the right side and did the same. The realization that I was facing the horror and humiliation of being raped was overshadowed only by the stark certainty of eventual death; but how long would it take that death to come; and by what means?

As this sadistic animal moved the knife down and cut my panties away, he had the look in his eyes of a hunter who was proudly dressing his prize kill. He leaned in and tried to kiss me, but I turned my head away and could not disguise my disgust. "Now is not the time," he said menacingly. I knew that what I did angered him and taking that slight bit of control away may very well have cost me my life at that moment.

He then reached down and took my nightshirt, wrapping it around my head and mouth. "I don't want you to be able to make any noise," he said. I pushed my jaw forward, hoping to secure breathing room once he was convinced I could not make noise. But, he was not satisfied. He then tied the shirt so tightly around my head that I thought I would lose consciousness.

Satisfied that I was properly silenced, he then pushed my body up on the bed and leaned me against the headboard. He began fondling me and making crude remarks about my body. The suddenly he grabbed me and thrust me over on my stomach. I tried to look up over my shoulder to see what he was trying to do. "Turn your head around," he barked. "You will not look at me and embarrass me that way. I mean it. If you look I will have to hurt you. I will tell you when you can look."

Lying on the bed, unable to see what this beast was about to do was like knowing a snake was in the room, but not being sure exactly where. I buried my face into my pillow and prayed that whatever he was about to do would be done quickly. He began muttering filthy statements; ordering me to move my body certain ways. I tried to tell him that I was bound and unable to move at all, but the shirt was tied so tightly he could not hear what I was saying. He pushed something up under my stomach that caused me to rise and felt like I might at any moment lose my balance and slide off.

As I struggled to keep my balance, the stranger seemed to become more excited. It was at this point that I realized what he was doing. It sickened me to the core of my being. He was masturbating. When it was obvious that he had completed his demented, obscene actions, I could feel him running the paper towels awkwardly across my lower back. I wanted to vomit.

The stranger was now standing somewhere behind me. I could hear him reach for a cigarette and light it. As if nothing had happened this vermin stood smoking a cigarette. I could smell the familiar odor of cigarette smoke as it wafted past my nose. I could not see him, but I could only imagine he was standing there reveling in his conquest.

I had my face buried in the pillow, praying that this may be the end and he would soon cut me loose and leave. Who was I kidding? How could I expect that such a disturbed, evil monster would ever be satisfied. I then felt the weight of this man on my back as he climbed on the bed and straddled me. What now?

Yea, though I walk through the valley of the shadow of death, I will fear no evil: for thou art with me; thy rod and thy staff they comfort me.
Psalm 23:4 KJV

Chapter 4

I struggled to get my head turned and mumbled through the nightshirt. "Can I look now?" I pleaded. Just as the words made their way out of my mouth, he grabbed my hair at the front of my head and pulled my head completely back. "Oh dear God," I said to myself. My worst fears were coming to past.

I heard him say, "Don't look." As he spoke he took the knife and placed it firmly against the right side of my neck. He then made a quick, but unyielding cut. I felt the sting of the blade slicing through the tender flesh of my neck, followed immediately by a searing pain. I could feel warm blood pouring out of my neck. He had cut me from the front to the back of my neck.

Instinctively, I began praying the Lord's Prayer. "Our Father who art in heaven, hallowed be thy name..." I then felt him grab my head and tilt it to the right as he then repeated his previous motion, slicing this time from the left side of my neck; again front to back. I knew he was carrying out what had been his plan all along, to kill me. However, my thoughts seemed focused less on my well-being, and more about praying for the safety of my son.

He kept making these deep, relentless gashes into my neck for what seemed like forever. I begged God to "make it stop." I blacked out briefly and when I awoke once again he was standing off to the side of the bed smoking a cigarette. "Are you still with me, bitch?" he said almost laughing.

He then jumped back on top of me and grabbed my head, yanking it back. I moaned and he realized I was actually still alive. He then plunged the knife into the side of my neck and drove it completely through to the other side. I felt as though my eyes were bulging out of the sockets. I could actually look down and see the knife protruding out of my throat.

Why wasn't I dead? I begged God to end it and let me die quickly. The stranger grabbed the knife and pulled it forward, turning it violently inside my throat. I could feel the blood filling my throat. Dear God, I am going to drown on my own blood.

I started trying to spit the blood out of my mouth into the nightshirt that was still tied around my mouth. The shirt quickly became soaked with my blood. My face and hair were dripping with my own wet, warm, sticky blood. He grabbed the knife and began thrusting it around inside my neck in an attempt to pull it out. He reached down and pulled the knife out from the opposite side he had driven it in. In the course of torturing me with the knife he had actually broken part of the knife off in my throat.

He was like a rabid animal, feeding off my pain and misery. He began to plunge the knife into my back over and over. I could feel it driving through my flesh and against the bones in my back. "Are you still with me, bitch," he said again. He suddenly took the knife and placed it at the back of my neck. Using his hand, he pounded it into the bone at the base of my neck. It felt as though he was cutting me into pieces. I could hear my neck crunching as he cut through the muscles and bone.

I continued to beg God to "take me now!" I sensed a voice telling me that it was not time. "You are not dead because it is not your time to go," the voice inside my head said. "You must suffer this, but soon you will have help." It was not like a voice, but more a thought that had been allowed inside my head as I was being savagely butchered. I could feel my mental "voice" saying, "No! I don't want help, I want to die now. Please let me die." I could not understand why I was not dead. I knew that if I would bring an end to this, it would only be by convincing him I was dead. Once again he grabbed my head back and sliced across my neck. As he dropped my head, I had lost so much blood that I became limp and unable to focus or even breath. I lay silent and pretended to be dead. He plunged the knife once more into my back and somehow I managed to lay lifeless. I kept my eyes closed and breathed as shallow as I possibly could. My mind shifted as if uncontrollably moving in a myriad of directions.

Thoughts of my mother and sisters and the times in my life that we shared quickly changed to mental theories of how I could have better protected myself and my son. I saw my son's face as he said goodnight and went to bed just a few hours earlier. Almost instinctively, I began to focus. I then turned my thoughts to the only thing that could make a difference at this point of uncertainly.

I began to pray. "Our Father who art in heaven, hallowed be thy name..." I lay dying, but the comfort that came upon me as I prayed was inexplicable; except I know now that God sent a blanket of love to cover my physical and emotional wounds. "Thy will be done, on earth as it is in heaven..." I continued. If I was destined to die that night, I wanted to be praying when I did.

Before he completed his hellish mission, this savage leaned over me and with my own blood took his finger and drew a smiley face at the base of my back. Satisfied that I was dead, the monster pushed my limp body off the bed into the floor. He then reached down and pulled a blanket up around my chin.

I heard him leave the room and as he went into the living room I heard him fumbling with the telephone. I did not hear him talk on the phone, only pick it up. A short time later I heard the back door close. He was gone.

I lay silent, afraid to make a sound for fear he would return. I knew I had to try and get up and move because I lay dying. My son was in his bedroom and this was the only chance I had in hours to get to him and gain confirmation that he was alright. I tried desperately to bring myself to an upright position, but it seemed I was almost paralyzed. Burning pain coursed through my arms and across my back as I pushed myself to roll over and get on my feet. Who was I kidding? "I am dying," I thought to myself.

I wanted to just separate myself from this agony and the thought of death seemed one opportunity. Once again, I realized that my son was only a few yards away at the other end of the house and I had to get to him; even if this was the last thing I did in my life. I managed to push my feet against the wall and brace my back against the bed. I struggled in agony to gain enough strength and momentum to force my body to an upright position. Twice I tried, twice I fell back down into the floor. On a third attempt I stood. I did not feel as though I had even enough physical strength to put one foot in front of the other and walk. I rested my body against the bedroom wall and felt unbearable pain in every part of my body. My chin lay on my chest because I could not lift my head. I gasped for breath and pushed my body down the wall toward the hallway.

I prayed fervently for God to give me the strength to make what any other time would have been a simple walk to the living room. I finally made my way into the living room and leaned against an entertainment center. There the phone lay only a few inches from my grasp. I could not lift my arms, they were still bound tightly with the electric cord.

I used my shoulder to knock the phone onto the floor in order to hopefully use my toes to dial 911. With a lunge I struck the phone and all at once both me and the phone fell to the floor. I struggled to breath, but knew if I had any chance I would have to get back on my feet and try to dial the phone.

Suddenly, I heard the sound of Nathan's feet running across the linoleum covered kitchen floor. It was the first true confirmation I had that my son was completely safe and unhurt since this nightmare had begun. In seconds he was by my side. "Mom, have you been stabbed? You are bleeding so badly," he exclaimed as he held me and tried to free my hands.

Feeling my son's touch was such a wonderful emotional reward, but physically I could not help but cry out each time he tried to console me and get me untied. "Is he still here," Nathan inquired? I assured him the monster had left the house. He then headed for the front door for help. Opening the door he briefly checked to be sure no one was loitering out side and he then bolted for the house next door. I drifted in and out of consciousness. By now my next door neighbor George and his mother, Paula, had arrived. I could hear someone talking to emergency personnel on the phone. Paula began cutting the cord that bound my hands. Though free, my arms were too weak to move from behind my back. Paula saw this and gently moved them from behind back and placed them at my side. Seeing how weak and injured I was, I heard her say almost under her breath, "Oh dear God." The pain was unbearable, but just as frightening was the difficulty I had trying to breath. I struggled for every breath. In what seemed like only a few minutes, the paramedics arrived. Moving everyone out of the way they began to work on me.

As he inspected my body for wounds and for points of priority attention, the paramedic apologized to me for having to do things that were hurting me. Those words were comforting to me. His apologetic tone seemed so contrasting to the barbaric treatment I had experienced at the hands of the sadistic animal who only minutes earlier gained great pleasure from systematically torturing me.

As the paramedic viewed my neck I heard him exclaim to his colleagues, "We don't have much time. We have got to get her out of here and to a hospital." He then warned me that he was forced to do the things he was doing and encouraged me to "hang in there." As a wrap was put around my neck and I was placed on a gurney, I hurt so badly that I begged for them to "please stop!"

I was told that I would be taken to a shock trauma hospital but it was not clear whether they could land a helicopter on US 13, the main highway just outside of my home, or perhaps attempt to transport me by ambulance. It was decided that an ambulance would be faster, so I was immediately loaded for transport to the hospital.

As they moved me outside to the ambulance I frantically attempted to cry out for Nathan. I could hear my then boyfriend, Andrew, calling out to me telling me he was there and how much he loved me. The paramedics allowed me to talk to Andrew briefly and with what little voice and breath I had left, I made him promise to take care of Nathan. He assured me he would keep Nathan with him.

I knew my son was safe, so I felt some comfort. But, now all I could think about as I was pushed into the ambulance was the evil, sadistic animal who had left my house secure in his belief I was dead. Was he somewhere nearby, watching the police and paramedics, planning his next move in response to me being alive?

When thou passest through the waters, I will be with thee; and through the rivers, they shall not overflow thee: when thou walkest through the fire, thou shalt not be burned; neither shall the flame kindle upon thee.
Isaiah 43: 2 (NIV)

Chapter 5

I stared at the ceiling of the ambulance as it sped out of the mobile home park and onto US 13. I felt every bump in the road, but by now all I wanted to do was sleep. I was hurting so badly, but my mind and body were absolutely exhausted.

I felt like I was ready to simply close my eyes and die. My body and soul were depleted and after fighting the most horrific battle of my life I was ready to just let go. As I let my eyes quietly close I recall hearing a voice inside my head scream at me, "You've made it this far, don't you dare give up now!" It was such a loud voice that it startled me and I immediately opened my eyes.

I lay battered and beaten, blood covered my body and soaked my hair, but I recall a certain peace that seemed out of place. I know now that God was there. He was allowing me to feel His presence. I was alive! I had beaten the Devil and I was bent on surviving this and making sure that somehow something good would come of it.

At the hospital in Salisbury, Maryland, I was about to encounter pain that would be close in intensity to that which I had just experienced. Right away the emergency room nurses and doctors began probing, injecting and cutting at my already limp and frail body.

The doctor informed me that my lungs were collapsing and he would need to place chest tubes that would be pushed in through each side of my upper body. He began slicing into my side and pushing a tube in. The pain was unbearable. As soon as he completed that task he moved to the other side. I was begging them, "Please, no more! Please stop."

What was happening to me was no more than an extension of the misery that the monster had perpetrated against me for hours at my home. What the doctors were doing was necessary to save my life, but only necessary because of what that inhuman animal had done.

In the midst of my anguish the nurses told me that my mother and my boyfriend were waiting to see me. My mother had been at work and was notified shortly after she started her shift at a Seaford department store. Andrew brought her to the hospital. I wanted to see them so badly, but I was not sure how I could even communicate with them.

The extensive damages to my throat left me immediately on life support with a breathing tube down my throat. As Mom and Andrew came into the room I could see they were visibly upset and Mom tried unsuccessfully to hide her tears of fear and concern.

I had heard the doctors tell the nurses that I would need to go to surgery. All I could think was, "Please give me something for this pain before I am forced to face the operating room." Thankfully the nurses brought a pain pump with morphine to allow me to self-medicate as needed for the pain. I motioned to my mother and Andrew to give me a paper and pen. I was determined to write as much as I could possibly write about the attack and the man who had tried to kill me. I took the pen in hand and frantically tried to write down a description of the man and information I believed would help police find him.

It was as if a million thoughts were rolling through my brain; all the while my body was on fire from the pain. By now two Delaware State Police Detectives had arrived and were standing over my bed. I became enraged when they reached down to take away the paper I was writing on. I wanted to desperately to scream at them, "Don't take the paper!," But the words would not come out.

As they showed me the paper I realized that they took it away because I was literally writing one message over the other in a mass of scribblings. I was becoming so disheartened. One of the detectives leaned over me and told me, "We will get this man. We promise you. If it is the last thing we ever do, we will find and arrest this man."

Looking into the eyes of these two police officers I could see they were truly sincere. This was not just rhetoric they had spewed out to try and comfort me. They meant what they said. This gave me even more determination to do what ever I could to help them. I felt so much better that these two officers were on my side.

Suddenly, my moment of contentment was rudely interrupted by the frightening words of the doctor who told the nurses, "We need to turn the respirator back on." This was my first knowledge that I had been placed on a respirator. My mind was now filled with images of my deathly ill grandmother lying in her bed, waiting to die while a respirator breathed for her. I made it clear after that I would never want a respirator used to keep me alive. If I could not breathe on my own I wanted them to let me go, I was now angry. My mother and the doctors could see I was becoming restless and frustrated. Able to see that my anger was coming from learning I was being placed on a respirator, the doctor tried to explain that I was not totally dependent on the respirator, but because of my injuries my lungs needed the support of the respirator.

His words fell on deaf ears and I became even more agitated. It was as if they were keeping me alive just to be sure I knew I was going to die. My mother came close to me and tried to comfort me. She told me I was not going to die. "You are breathing on your own, honey. You just need a little help for the time being, until you are strong enough to do it all by yourself," she said.

I am not sure if I believed my mother, or if I was just so tired and realized it did no good to fight. Whatever the reason, I dropped my resistance. Though I was tired I was scared to go to sleep. Looking back it is completely ludicrous, but at the time I still believed the monster could still get to me if I was careless and fell asleep.

After all, it was because I decided to go back to sleep after he came to my home knocking on the door the first time that left me so vulnerable. As I lay in that emergency room hospital bed all I could picture in my mind was his horrible face as he peered into the window of my backdoor. Just looking into his eyes I knew he was evil; he was the symbol of Satan himself.

Why was it not possible that this man could find me no matter where I was, no matter how safe it seemed, and kill me? I was surrounded by medical professionals, police detectives and my mother and boyfriend. I was in the safe confines of a major hospital. Still I was overwhelmed with paranoia. I could not feel safe. This animal still had control of me. I was locked in my own internal hell and this madman was the gatekeeper.

Ye shall not fear them: for the LORD your God He shall fight for you.
Deuteronomy 5-3:22

Chapter 6

My mouth was dry. I could hear the sounds of machines pumping and the annoying sound of air hissing near my head. There were also the sounds of people moving about almost like ghosts from here to there, whispering to one another. As my eyes opened I eventually recognized that I was in the Intensive Care Unit of the hospital.

Like a horrendous flood of morbid realization, I instantly began recalling bits and pieces of events that brought me to this place. I started being overtaken by a feeling of desperation and anxiety. "Where is my mother? Where is Nathan?" I began asking frantically. I was not in pain as I had been prior to falling off to sleep; but I was wracked with fear and angst. I knew I would feel so much better with my family on each side of my hospital bed. My voice was weak and barely audible.

I wanted to see my mother and I needed to see my son. Nathan had been in that house while I was being tortured. He may have seen this monster. I had no way of knowing if he was safe. "I want to see my son," I demanded.

The nurse informed me that I could not see my son. She told me that the police had him in hiding until they were sure it was safe for him to return to my family. Although I may have been happy to hear he was being taken care of, I still needed to see him myself. I needed to see him and confirm that he was safe and unharmed.

I wanted to see my son, but did my son need to see me? I had lost sight of the fact that I was badly injured and must look horrific. I had intravenous lines running into both hands, a heart monitor beeping over my head, a respirator helping me to breathe, a catheter, a feeding tube, circulation warps around both legs, staples and stitches in my ears and neck, and two drainage tubes protruding from my neck. It would be horrible for a child to see their mother like this. But, I did not take that into consideration; I just needed to see and hold my son.

Suddenly I had a thought that sent a shock of fear throughout my body and to the core of my soul. Maybe Nathan was not alright. Maybe these people wanted me to get better before they told me some awful news about my son. I became frantic. "When will this nightmare end?," I cried to myself.

I had become obsessed with asking about my son and pleading for him to be brought to me. When Andrew visited me in the ICU he reinforced what I had been told and promised me that Nathan was safe and doing fine. To help control my fear, he gave me a picture of Nathan that he kept in his wallet and taped it to a side rail of my bed.

I finally had the breathing tube removed and my throat was raw and sore. My vocal ability was limited to a whisper.

"What day is it?" I asked Andrew with a voice that must have been difficult for him to understand. If it was hard for him to interpret what I was saying he never let on. "It is Wednesday," he said. "You have been here for two days, honey."

The days to follow seemed to be almost surrealistic and days mixed with nights as I was still being sedated and treated for my painful wounds. At a certain point I was told I could be moved to a regular room and leave the ICU. To anyone else this would seem promising news, but to me all I could think about was how much more open and available a traditional hospital room could be. How could I be guaranteed safety?

I was being fed through a feeding tube, but the thought of food did not appeal to me anyway. I was tired, but determined to get out of the hospital. I began to maneuver myself around the hospital room, slowly gaining the strength to keep myself up on my feet. My mother would come to the hospital each day and bathe me, while Andrew seemed to spend every waking hour at my side.

He would pull a chair up close to the hospital bed and hold my hand while I slept and rub my feet when I was feeling uncomfortable. My sisters were taking care of Nathan and one at a time they would come to visit me each day. I could not have gotten through this without the support of my family and friends.

When I was taken out of the ICU I was placed in a private room and police guards were posted at my door. I was only allowed visits from my family because they warned me of the need to keep track of every person that came to my room. Still my son was not able to come and see me. This continued to be a point of misery for me. How could they expect me to get better without allowing me to see my son? I began receiving daily visits from the Delaware State Police detectives who were investigating my case I wanted to help them all I could and answer all of their questions because I wanted this man to be caught.

I was able to recall things from the night that I was attacked that helped the investigation. I vividly recall seeing the stranger touching a water glass, holding one of my kitchen knives, using my cigarette case and rifling through my pocketbook. Certainly there had to be fingerprints somewhere in my home.

The detectives took my fingerprints to allow them to deduct them from any other prints they found in the house. Then they repeatedly asked me if I may have seen this man somewhere before. They asked about my ex-husband and my ex-boyfriends. I was becoming frustrated because the more I tried to convince them that it was a complete stranger who attacked me, the more they seemed to push about the possibility it may have been someone I knew. "If this is someone you know, you can tell us," one officer said. "We can protect you. We can make sure he never hurts you again."

Finally, I made it as clear as I could to the detectives. "I know what these people look like," I said firmly. "The man who broke into my home and attacked me is someone I have never seen in my life." Finally they shifted their line of questioning and did not return to asking me if I somehow knew the man.

The feeding tube was removed and I was told to slowly start attempting to eat. I tried ice chips at first, but could barely get them down without choking. Eventually I graduated to small amounts of baby food. I was starting to get my appetite back, but the baby food was all I could handle. My throat was still extremely sensitive and gave me a lot of discomfort.

I continued to speak in a whisper and I would get out of breath trying to finish a sentence. After a few days out of ICU I finally got enough strength to stand in the bathroom and wash my face on my own. Andrew helped me to the bathroom and then closed the door, leaving me alone in a room for the first time since my attack. As the heavy bathroom door closed I could feel my chest tighten and my heart begin to beat quickly as I struggled to convince myself that I wasn't alone. People were gathered just on the other side of the door. My mind shifted very abruptly as I moved my eyes to the large mirror that hung over the sink just in front of me. The woman who stared back at me was someone I did not know. Her battered, scarred face was drawn and pale. It was me, but me as I had never imagined.

I was ugly and I even frightened myself as I looked into the mirror. Tears streamed down my face as I stood there holding in the disappointment and devastation. "How can I learn to deal with this?" I thought to myself.

The tubes and stitches had been removed, but my eye was drooping from severe nerve damage and my ears and both sides of my face were numb. My shoulder and right arm were constantly burning with pain and I had difficulty using them. Now, along with the physical misery and pain I had to endure, I was facing an emotional devastation that I feared would cause me to lose my mind.

Finally, after what seemed forever, police allowed Nathan to visit me at the hospital. Seeing him safe and smiling brought me my first sense of comfort. I hugged him like we had been separated for years. I was so thankful that God had protected him and he had not been hurt during the horrific events that took place that night in our home. Feeling him in my arms made me realize how important it was for me to try to move forward and recover from this nightmare.

*And he said unto him, arise, go thy way: thy faith
hath made thee whole.*
Luke 17:19

Chapter 7

As I languished in the hospital, my life seemed to have come to a halt. I was hoping I would soon be released, but then I would have to deal with where I would go to live. I would certainly not go back to the home where I had been attacked; that was out of the question. I decided I would move in with Andrew and try to sell my home in Laurel.

I could not stop thinking about the fact that the monster who left me for dead was still out there somewhere. He was still able to hurt my family, or come back to finish the job he started on me. My wounds were still fresh and my memories were crystal clear. I prayed they would catch the man who had in the course of a few horrible hours stolen my ability to feel safe. Though moving in with Andrew gave me a sense of security, I was still petrified about being left alone. So, before Andrew went to work he would take me to my sister's house and pick me up in the afternoon on his way home from work.

I was literally scared of my own shadow. Even with Andrew there, I would often be afraid to go to sleep for fear I would wake to find a stranger had slipped into the house. I wanted someone standing outside the bathroom door as I took a shower or bath.

I hated that I had been robbed of my independence, of my ability to feel safe and to live anything close to a normal life. I believed that God had brought me through this; I thanked him daily for saving me and protecting my son. But, I could not understand why any of this happened at all.

As I prayed I felt an assurance that God was in the midst of all of this turmoil and confusion. I believed that as hard as this was to deal with, God felt I was strong enough to see this through. I would do whatever it would take to see that this man was apprehended and unable to hurt anyone again. I had plenty of time to think; unfortunately, too much time to think

At times I would find myself obsessed with thinking about how much I hated the man who had attacked me and how badly I wanted to see him dead. Other times I would actually start to feel sorry for him as I contemplated what may have happened to him as a child that caused him to become such a sadistic and narcissistic barbarian.

Along with an ever-present feeling of helplessness, I began to question if I would ever get to the point that I would be able to stop depending on people to help me do the chores that at one time were second nature to me. I had to have people help dry me after a bath and help me put on my clothes. I felt like an invalid, a helpless child.

I was always so independent. I was not the type of person who asked for help easily. Among my many fears was the fear that I had been hurt so badly that if faced with danger, I may no longer have the physical strength to fight back, to protect my self. I was beginning to recognize the power of negative thoughts. I had learned many years ago that there was great healing in the power of positive confirmation that came as the result of a belief and faith in God. I was not about to allow some mentally ill freak to rob me of the ability to lead a normal life and be happy. He tried to take my life, but he failed. I believe he failed because God had other plans for me.

I had to find the strength to rally back from this onslaught of negative thinking. If I was to truly believe the promises of God's love, I had to trust Him and believe He had a plan. I had to muster the courage to fight back and regain my life. I had to pray and pray hard!

My consistent inability to feel safe, even surrounded by family and friends, led me to have Andrew install a home security system and purchase a gun for me. I had a licensed 9mm handgun, and I took private lessons on how to properly use it. It was big and felt overwhelming and heavy in my tiny hands. I suppose everyone who acquires a gun for protection has to ask his or herself, "Would you be prepared to actually use this weapon if you felt threatened?" For me the answer seemed frighteningly simple, "Yes."

There was to be one more source of protection brought into my life; it was a big rock of a Rottweiler dog named, "Cujo." This dog was gorgeous. Her sleek, black fur was close to her body and I fell in love with her almost immediately. She was great company to me when the inevitable came to pass and Andrew no longer could spend every day taking me back and forth to my sister's house. I had to start a path toward some sense of independence. But it would not prove to be easy.

I had purchased Cujo with aspirations of raising her to become my guard dog. She became like a second child. I played with her and spoiled her; she loved me and week by week she became more and more protective of me. I had made the right choice. This dog quickly became my personal protector. As I tended to the awkward and extremely tiring routine of what had become my life, the police were also busy. The investigation had finally produced results. People in the community had become so engrossed in my case and were extremely troubled by how such a senseless, violent, random and heinous act could happen to someone who was not unlike their wife, their daughter, their sister, or even themselves. Police began to receive huge volumes of tips through anonymous phone calls to the State Police at Troop 5, in Bridgeville, and through the statewide "Crime Stoppers" phone line. One call was particularly interesting. On October 1, 1995, just a few weeks after my attack, a neighbor living in the mobile home park near my home called Delaware State Police at about 10:30 pm to report a suspicious man out in the yard of my home.

She said the man was sitting in a red pick-up truck outside my home with a candle burning on the top of his truck. A State Trooper was sent to my house and interviewed the neighbor who made the call. After getting a description of the truck and the man, it was broadcast as a police bulletin and police in the area started looking for this mysterious man and his red truck. Within two hours state police found a truck matching the description in the parking lot of the Oasis Truck Stop, on US 13, just a little over a mile south of the mobile home park where I lived. The state trooper interviewed the owner of the truck and immediately recognized that he matched the description I had given of my attacker. A police sketch artist had made a composite sketch based on my recollection of the man who had attacked me. The composite sketch was found inside the man's truck.

At the truck stop that night police found that the man, identified as Leo DeSilva, a Maryland automobile mechanic, had cut the composite sketch out of the local newspaper and taped it to the window of his truck. DeSilva also had a candle burning on the top of his truck. The strange circumstances and the close resemblance to my assailant led police to take DeSilva to the Laurel Police Station where he was photographed and interviewed.

During questioning DeSilva did not deny he was at my house earlier that night. He said his daughter lived in the mobile home park and he had been driving back and forth from his home in Lanham, Maryland to visit her. He said earlier that night he had stopped by my house with a lit candle to hold a private vigil to pray for my safe recovery and the apprehension of the person who had committed the crime. A day after the interview state police contacted me and asked if I would take a look at some photographs. I agreed and they showed me six pictures of different men. One face jumped out at me – it was the face of DeSilva. There was no question in my mind that this was my attacker. I told police I was absolutely certain that this was the man who had beaten and stabbed me.

Everything seemed to be happening so fast. After all of the pain and emotional misery I had been forced to deal with following the attack, I was now dealing with a different trauma; the possibility of once again facing this demon.

With the new developments coming in my case I was hearing more from the chief investigators, detectives Sgt. Doug Hudson and Sgt. Robert A. Hudson, II. They had interviewed DeSilva, but kept details from me until after I had the chance to view the photo lineup.

Police were becoming convinced they had the man in custody who had tried to kill me. I started to learn more about what took place during the interviews. Police told me that DeSilva never denied committing the crime. At one point during discussions with police DeSilva even offered up his apologies for what had happened to me. Though falling short of legal standards, I felt this was as good as a confession.

Probably the most startling thing to come out of the early interviews police had with DeSilva was something he did which threw police for a loop. In the midst of the interview, DeSilva requested police to allow him to fill out an employment application. He told them he wanted to be a state trooper.

This made absolutely no sense to the police, but they obliged him and brought an application. After DeSilva completed the application, police noticed something very bizarre. At the base of the last page of the application under his signature, DeSilva had drawn a "happy face" eerily similar to the bloody happy face that was left at the base of my back by the attacker.

Police had purposely left the information about the bloody "happy face" out of press releases and other statements to the media. Only the attacker would know about this heinous, bloody signature. I was becoming more and more convinced that this was the man. I just wanted to hear him say something, that would be the final piece of evidence to assure me it was him. I was told by police that I would need to come to the state police troop to identify DeSilva and make sure there was no question in my mind that he was my attacker. At the troop, I was told I could do the identification via video camera, or go into a room and see him face-to-face. My heart was racing and I felt as though my legs would give out under me.

I knew I would never be satisfied unless I saw this man face-to-face and heard him speak. I needed to be completely sure. I did not want to send an innocent man to prison. Against my own emotions and in a state of total fear, I requested to do the identification in person.

Entering the room I immediately saw him. He was shackled and dressed in orange prison garb. As our eyes met, I became nauseous. His eyes were stone cold. I felt the same fear that I had felt the night I was tortured and left for dead. "I need to hear him speak," I told the detective standing next to me. As DeSilva spoke, each word gave me increased confirmation that this was the man who tried to murder me. I wanted to leave that room immediately.

The next night detectives called and said they needed Nathan to come to the state police troop and do an identification. Police were aware that Nathan had also briefly seen the man on the night of the attack when he had gone into the bedroom to check on him. When I told him what he needed to do it was obvious to me that Nathan was visibly apprehensive.

On the ride over to the state police troop Nathan kept asking if he would have to be in the room with the man in order to identify him. I could not answer his question,I really did not know how this would be done. One thing was for sure, I would fight any action that would cause my son to be forced to revisit the fear and horror of that night. I wanted confirmation that DeSilva was the attacker, but not at the expense of my son's emotional well-being.

Seeing Nathan's anxiety I felt powerless to comfort and reassure him when we were dealing with something that was without a doubt the most horrible, life-changing ordeal in either of our lives. Then, I realized that I was trying to be the "hero," the savior. Of course I could not give my son, or myself for that matter, the comfort and assurance we needed at such a dismal time in our lives.

I needed to take this burden to God. I put my hand in Nathan's hand and began to pray. I prayed that God would calm him and relieve his anxiety and fear. I prayed that God would give my son the courage it took to face this ordeal and do the right thing, no matter what the outcome.

After praying Nathan was so much more relaxed, still nervous, but not as frantic as earlier. He then asked, "Mom, what if I can't identify him?" I simply told him to do the best he could and if he wasn't sure, just be honest and tell the police.

At the state police troop we were escorted into a room where Nathan was given a seat. The detectives brought out a group of pictures and laid them in front of him. I stood behind Nathan so that I would not inadvertently look at a picture while he was trying to pick one out on his own.

He studied the pictures one by one and it was evident from the way he moved his head from side to side and squinted his eyes that he was having a problem. He was trying, but it was just not working. He looked at the detective and said, "I am not sure. All of these pictures have the guys looking at me. I only saw the man from the side. If I could see them from the side I am sure I would be able to identify the man."

The detectives left the room and returned a short time later with photos of the assortment of men at a side view. Looking over the photos, Nathan pointed to one and said, "That's him. I am sure. I remember how he had his hair combed straight back." It was the same man I picked out – Doug DeSilva.

I am sure there are many times in life when a parent is proud of their child. When he hits his first baseball in Little League; when he brings home a good report card, or when he takes time to help another person. But, what Nathan did in that small room at the state police headquarters will always be one of my most treasured moments of parental pride. My young son took on a weight that any man would find difficult, and he helped make sure my attacker faced justice. My son was my hero.

No temptation has seized you except what is common to man. And God is faithful; he will not let you be tempted beyond what you can bear. But when you are tempted, he will also provide a way out so that you can stand up under it.
1 Corinthians 10:13

Chapter 8

I know that regardless of how bad things are, there is always someone else who is suffering a fate far worse. But, when your life is shred apart and you are suddenly faced with a deep-seated belief that you can never truly feel safe again, it is hard to comprehend anything but despair.

I know people take all kinds of self-defense courses to help prepare for the potential of being confronted by an attacker. But, that training does not prepare you for the aftermath of a brutal attack. We do not live our lives considering that a compete stranger may break into our home in the middle of the night and try to murder us. That is something that only happens to other people living in big, dangerous cities. It is something that only happens in the movies.

But life does not necessarily occur by our own design. It takes twists and turns as unplanned circumstances present themselves. We should be aware that circumstances in life can sometimes take an undesired, unfair turn, but we are never prepared for that. I was certainly far from prepared for the hand life had suddenly and maliciously dealt me.

I have often heard it said that God will not put more on you than you can handle. I have also heard many people say "what doesn't kill you will make you stronger." In either case, I found great solace in my life's predicament through these mantras.

It seemed impossible to consider my life from a normal perspective. I was now forced to deal with not only the physical brutality that had befallen me, but emotional scars that created a personality within me that I did not recognize.

I was short tempered, on edge constantly waiting for something else bad to happen to me. I was driven by a sense of justice that bordered on vengeance. I wanted to hurt someone like I had been hurt. Gone was the innocent girl whose daily worries consisted of the fears of being late for work or getting a speeding ticket. I now longed for the normal frustrations of daily life.

"Oh, my God," I thought. "I have become a victim." These words burned through my mind like a white- hot branding iron. I could not allow my situation to make me become a weak, cowering, self-loathing shell of myself. I would not let the actions of one man change me into something I did not want to become. But, it was happening.

I recalled the words to an old spiritual song that I had sung countless times in church. The lyrics really spoke to me. "Where could I go, oh where could I go. Seeking a refuge for my soul. Needing a friend to save me in the end. Where could I go but to the Lord."

If I was ever going to make any sense out of the bizarre, physically and mentally draining events that had occurred, I would need to lean on the Lord and not my own understanding. Try as I may, I could not shake this feeling of overwhelming tragedy and hurt.

I prayed to God when I lay on the bedroom floor of my home, beaten, ravaged and bloody. I prayed because I knew that I was on the verge of certain death. God responded and saved me. I believe this. I truly believe that in my darkest, most painful hours, God held me and protected me from the death sentence being carried out by a complete stranger.

Now, as I began to heal physically, I realized that my wounds were much deeper than flesh. I was now wounded emotionally – wounded spiritually. Just as much as I needed God as I lay bleeding and lifeless on the floor of that bedroom, I needed God now. As I try to fight the propensity to allow the savagery of what this man did to me to manifest into a desire for vengeance, I needed God to help me find peace. I began to pray and seek God's wisdom. I know now that God wanted even more for me than to simply survive my attack. He wanted me to live each day of my life unafraid and able to recognize that with Jesus all things are possible. I was now determined to use each new day as an opportunity to recognize how blessed I have been and to live my life not so much as a survivor, but more as a conqueror.

I started making sure I found time to spend in prayer each day. I called on God when I faced what I believed to be my last moments on earth, and he responded. Now I wanted to talk to God and seek His counsel as I tried to piece my life back together and move forward. I would find the strength and with God's help, begin to face life void of this nagging sense of hate that seemed to be attempting to keep me in bondage.

My pledge to spend more time in counsel with God proved to be a very wise decision. I soon found that the wheels of justice turn very slowly. I was confident nothing would happen as quickly as I would like, so I prayed God would give me the ability to accept what I had no control over. Medical bills began to stream in and I was out of work and unable to understand how I would pay them. I was living with Andrew, but my frame of mind and stressed conditions probably made me a less than desirable housemate. I had a home, but I was afraid to live there. I knew I would need to try and get my mobile home repaired and consider selling it.

A cleaning company had come in to attempt the cleanup at my home. They were successful in ridding the inside of the home of the fingerprint dust that was used by police investigators on much of my household items. However, they were unable to get the blood out of the carpet. I was told that due to health concerns, the cleaning company could not do a carpet replacement. I suppose I can understand their rationale, but it still left me feeling somewhat offended. I was able to get a contractor to come in an do the carpet replacement. Actually, picking out the carpet was good therapy for me. I was finally able to take control of at least one aspect of my life.

My sister helped me re-paint the bedroom where most of the attack had occurred. Once that was done and the carpet replaced, all evidence was gone that would remind anyone of the horror that took place only a couple of months earlier. But, this did not influence me to reconsider selling the house and living elsewhere. No amount of paint or new carpet would help me to forget what had happened to me within those walls.

I received word from the courts that DeSilva's attorney was requesting a mental evaluation for his client. I can certainly see where the actions of this man were overtly sadistic and lacking any level of humanity. But, it would crush me to think he would find a way to escape justice through a plea of insanity. The man who did this to me was ruthless and mean, but he was not crazy.

I would now be faced with waiting to find the results of his mental evaluations. This on top of the fact that I had to wait to hear about whether he was HIV positive. I learned that the first forms I signed to seek the request for an HIV/AIDS test had somehow been misplaced, so the process took even longer.

Finally, I received word that DeSilva was found competent to stand trial and I would get my day in court and a chance at justice. I also received word that the HIV tests came back as negative. For me this was two pieces of good news.

A hearing was scheduled and I made sure to be at the courthouse for the proceedings. I sat in the empty courtroom for what seemed like hours. Finally, I left and went to find out why there was such a delay. I was frustrated to learn that I had been waiting in the wrong courtroom. All that time and no one thought to tell me that I needed to be in another room.

Suffice to say, I missed the proceedings. They were very short; only long enough for DeSilva to plead "Not guilty." But, I was not able to be there. I did not have the chance to stare this man in the face and remind him why he was sitting in prison. I wanted him to see me in a different light. I wanted him to see me strong and determined, not like the beaten, bloody woman that he had held hostage and under his control.

I am sure it was not intentional for the state prosecution to overlook me sitting in the wrong courtroom, or for papers to get misplaced. But, these types of things left me feeling so alone in all of this confusion. I recognize the legal process is a job to these people and to them it is a daily repetition. But, for me it was all I had to depend on for any sense of justice.

The court staff may do this everyday, but I do not. This was something I never wanted, but now that I had no choice but to deal with it, I wanted to be a part of it. I wanted to be a priority. I wanted justice.

The great trials which your eyes saw and the signs and the wonders and the mighty hand and the outstretched arm by which the LORD your God brought you out. So shall the LORD your God do to all the peoples of whom you are afraid.
Deuteronomy 7:18-20

Chapter 9

It is difficult to explain how trauma affects an individual. It is something that I wrestle with daily. As I said earlier, people are not prepared for the aftermath of a traumatic event such as a vicious physical attack. Even after being released from the hospital and sensing that I was slowly recovering from the massive physical injuries I had suffered, there was something transpiring within my mental processes. I found myself so afraid. I began to actually feel the same fears and desperation that were present during the attack whenever I would recall, or otherwise be reminded of what had happened to me. I actually began to question whether I may lose my mind. I certainly wondered if I would ever feel safe again.

The stress takes a toll on everyone: family and friends. The misery that had been thrust on me seemed to bleed over into every aspect of my life. Nathan and I were filled with so much anger, hate, and repressed emotions; neither one of us had any idea of how to deal with these emotions.

The emotional roller coaster was particularly impacting life at Andrew's house. There seemed to be few nights when an argument did not break out and someone had their feelings hurt. I knew this was not good for Andrew, Nathan or me. Nathan and I began to seek counseling. We would go to a counseling session and things would be fine for a couple of days. Then out of nowhere there would suddenly be arguments and temper tantrums between us and anyone else in the immediate area.

Day by day I began to realize that any future plans with Andrew were not to be. The stress and misery had driven a wedge between us. I knew for everyone's sake I had to make other living arrangements. The horror that came as a result of my attack was not limited to that one night of hell. It seemed to follow me like a storm cloud.

I moved out of Andrew's home and into the home of one of my sisters and her family. I had planned to be there for only a few days, but they made me feel so much at home that we remained there. However, my fears and frustrations traveled along with me.

In addition to my Rottweiller, Cujo, and carrying the 9mm handgun, I also purchased canisters of pepper spray. I carried the protective spray in my pocketbook and even clipped a canister on my pajamas and slept with it every night. I was doing everything I could to become less vulnerable, less unprepared.

I was overwhelmed with a sense of impending doom. I had not forgotten the words spoken by the man who attacked me. He had convinced me that there may be another person that was outside of my home that night. Would this other, mystery man seek to finish the job his partner had started. Would he track me down and kill me? Would I ever feel that my family and I were safe?

Although I met with a number of counselors who attempted to help me cope with some of the emotions I was feeling, I recognized that the fear and frustration was becoming entrenched within my very being. Once again, I found myself seeking a closer relationship with God. It was only during those times when I prayed and worked hard to lean on His understanding that I felt any sense of true hope.

I was convinced that regardless of how confusing and completely senseless all of this was, God had a plan. I had to believe that by dealing with my sordid issues based on a trust in God, I would somehow be able to find one day that there was a method to all this madness.

I was finally able to return to my job at a local insurance agency. I knew it would be difficult to stay on top of my finances, but at least I was aware of who needs to be paid and when they are to be paid. It was also great to know that there was some steady money coming in.

Before long, I was informed that I would be dealing with painful reconstructive surgery. My doctor said the process involves re-opening the many stab wounds on my neck and then surgically closing them. I was told after this surgery my scars would be minimally visible.

I knew that the day would soon come when I would see Douglas DeSilva in the courtroom. I was so excited to consider being there void of the glaring scars I now possessed. Having this reconstructive surgery would be one more opportunity to show him that with the help of God, he was unable to render me helpless and broken. It would be worth the pain of the surgery to accomplish this.

But this opportunity came with a price. The pain of the surgery and the removal of the new stitches left me feeling like there was little left that I could handle in terms of physical misery. My physical and mental capacities were being tested to their limits. How much more of this torture was I able to endure? It is as if this man continued to hurt me, even while he was behind prison bars. I had grown so weary of this emotional storm that I dealt with daily. I wanted this all to be put behind me. I wanted my life back. I wanted to laugh again. I wanted to do all the normal things I used to do. I wanted to go shopping without constantly looking around to be sure no one is following me. When would I finally feel normal again? I think about this maniac who attacked me and though I am confident he is behind bars, I can't help but spend my days expecting him to suddenly bolt out from behind any door in the house and confront me. I hate this man and I want to hurt him like he has hurt me. Other times I realize that I still fear this man. All of this frustrates me because it means he still has power over me. Sitting behind steel bars he is able to continue wreaking havoc in my life.

How did he get this way? What happened to him in life that created such evil within his soul? Why would someone willfully seek to hurt someone so viciously if they themselves had not somehow been hurt? I think of him as a child and wonder what his young life may have been like? Was he abused? Was he bullied? Why does he do the things he does? There must be a reason.

Why is it so important for me to feel the need to rationalize an irrational situation? Why do I so desperately need to feel there is an answer to unanswerable questions. Why me? Why out of all the people who live in Laurel, Delaware, did he choose me as prey? Then there is the biggest question of all – does any of it really matter?

I suppose it would have been better for me to use less energy questioning the rationale behind my situation and more energy trying to change things that were within my control. I needed to get my mobile home ready for sale. Since moving out from Andrew's house I stored all of my personal belongings there.

Between recuperating from my reconstructive surgery and a recent snow storm, I had been unable to get back into the home to do any work. One evening I decided to check my phone messages by calling the answering machine at the mobile home. I immediately recognized that the answering machine was not working, so I needed to find out out why.

Before going to the house I stopped to check the mail at the entrance to the mobile home park. A former neighbor was also checking his mail. He stopped to exchange small talk and asked if I had been successful in selling my mobile home. After telling him that I had no luck in finding a buyer, he showed a look of surprise. He said he had seen someone going into the backdoor of my home earlier and assumed I had sold the home and was moving my things out.

I immediately called Andrew and asked him to meet me at my home. When we approached the back door, it was noticeable that there had been a break-in. The door was ajar and the frame was broken. We called the police and waited outside for them. When police arrived the officer entered the home with a police dog. Inside for just a few seconds they both emerged and told us that there was no one inside. The officer then asked me to come in and check the inside of the home.

As I stepped inside the living room of my home my heart sank. It was obvious at first glance everything was gone. Someone had broken in and stolen my stove, refrigerator, stereo, microwave, VCR and all the living room furniture. It was apparent through closer inspection that not only did they steal all of my belongings, they had actually slept in the home and left beer bottles and cigarettes throughout. Someone had been so brazen as to urinate in the bathtub and leave vomit laying inside the bathroom sink.

In talking to neighbors it appeared that because I had a "For Sale" sign in the window of my home and I was not living in there, they were not suspicious about the activities that had transpired. No one considered it unusual when over the course of a week individuals were seen loading a truck with my belongings. They, like my neighbor at the mailbox, assumed this was simply associated with the possible sale of the home. I went from room to room and became more and more disheartened. All of my personal belongings had been dumped in the middle of the floor and someone had rummaged through them. In my son's bedroom all of his toys and clothes were gone and his baseball card collection was strewn across the bedroom floor. I fell to my knees and began to sob. Just as I had started to convince myself that things in my life could not possibly get any worse, they suddenly did.

I stood in the living room of what was once my home; what was once my solace from the troubles of the outside world. I looked around the rooms and saw nothing that reminded me of the warmth and peace that my son and I had only a few months earlier enjoyed here.

Thieves had taken advantage of my life's lowest point. As my eyes moved from corner to corner I noticed something very interesting. Along the wall next to my back door, amid the scattered debris, was a small stack of boxes and my television. This was stacked and awaiting a future pickup. The thieves were planning to come back. Andrew and I decided we would stay at the house and be there when, and if, they returned. This time if there was going to be a crime at my home I was going to be waiting and ready.

Therefore I am well content with weaknesses, with insults, with distresses, with persecutions, with difficulties, for Christ's sake; for when I am weak, then I am strong.
2 Corinthians 12:10

Chapter 10

Andrew and I spent the night inside my mobile home, armed with a 9mm handgun. Fortunately, or unfortunately, as the case may be, no one showed up. All through the night I found it difficult to sleep. Though I was secure knowing that Andrew was there with me, I could not help but feel that this robbery at my home was somehow connected to DeSilva. Was the break-in and robbery simply meant to be a message to me from DeSilva. Was he letting me know that I was never outside of his reach? Or was this just a sick coincidence? Regardless of the circumstances, it did little to boost my sense of security.

The following day Andrew and I remained in the mobile home with no vehicles in the yard, hoping someone would show up and we could catch them in the act. Later in the afternoon I decided to call in a food order at a nearby restaurant. I called my friend Gwen, who lived near my mobile home to take me to her house so I could call in the order and she could take me to pick it up.

After I arrived at her house and made the food order, her phone rang. Gwen answered the phone and almost immediately became hysterical. She shouted to me that it was a neighbor calling who witnessed Andrew armed with his gun, chasing two men from my mobile home. They had come back just after I left.

I immediately yelled to Gwen that I was going to go after them. We both jumped out the door and into her van. As we were climbing into the van I saw one of Gwen's neighbors in his yard. I screamed for him to call 911 and tell them there was an emergency; I gave him my address as we sped off. We drove toward my mobile home, less than two minutes away. As we approached I saw Andrew running behind two younger men. I ordered Gwen to drive toward the men.

I told her to roll down her window and I handed her a can of the pepper spray that had become a constant companion. I rolled my window down and locked the door. As Gwen drove up beside the young man who was now running next to my side of the van, I called to him and as he turned to look at me, I sprayed him directly in the face with the pepper spray. He ran and fell into the grass.

Gwen immediately turned the vehicle around and went back toward the second runner. She pulled up beside him and did just as I had done earlier. The spray struck the running man right on target and he, like his partner, tumbled to the ground.

Both men suddenly got back on their feet and ran frantically toward a wooded area near the mobile home development. Gwen drove her van to where Andrew was working his way in pursuit of the two partially blinded men. She slowed down and Andrew hopped into the van and we headed after the men.

Within a couple of minutes state police with a police dog arrived on scene and we told them where the two men had last been seen heading into the woods. The police went on foot with the dog to hunt for the men. Meanwhile, a passing motorist who had just come into the development stopped and told Andrew that one of the men had run between mobile homes and was still in the development.

Andrew left with the man and was able to pick up the thief's footprints in the snow. He followed the footprints to a home in the development and yelled for the man to come out. A woman came to the door and ordered Andrew off her property. It turned out that she was the mother of the ringleader of the gang of men who had robbed my home. She said her son was not home, but Andrew told her he knew she was lying and she needed to send her son out.

Within a couple of minutes her son came to the door, but apparently having been maced by me and seeing the gun in

Andrew's hand, he refused to come outside until the police arrived. Police did arrive very shortly and had the other man in custody as well.

Andrew and I followed the police officers back to the Delaware State Police Troop in nearby Bridgeville. There we gave our account of what had transpired to police detectives. The two men were in other rooms, also giving statements. State Police Detective Tony Wallace came out and told me we could go home. He said he would call me the next day to let me know where we stood with the case.

As we headed back home both Andrew and I had a great sense of pride. We had stood our ground and decided that we would not allow me to become just another victim of a senseless crime. I felt so excited that I had maintained control and not simply lay down and played the victim card. We had helped police catch the men who stole everything I owned. Although I still felt violated, I also felt that I had helped carry out some immediate justice.

The next day Detective Wallace called as he had promised. He told me that one of the men we had chased had turned on his partner and named the other man, "Steve," as the one who had actually been directly involved in the theft of my property.

It seems that Steve later confessed to police and told them what he had done. He said that he had broken into my home and loaded my belongings in a truck. He traveled to locations in two states offering my household items for sale. He told the unsuspecting potential buyers about my ordeal and said that he was my boyfriend and I had asked him help me sell my property.

Detective Wallace said my property had been sold to people from several different locations and it was unlikely, outside of a couple of the major appliances, I would see any of it again. He was right. Over the next few weeks police returned my kitchen stove and refrigerator. But, as I had assumed, these items came back in far worse shape than when they left. Apparently there is not great care taken in handling stolen merchandise.

Eventually, the culprits went to court. Before it was over there had been five people charged in the robbery of my home. I had made insurance claims on my property, but there was no way to replace the sentimental items that had been taken from the home. I would have to be satisfied that the guilty people had been caught and that no one got physically hurt in the process.

It was now once again time for me to turn my attention to the court proceedings involving Douglas DeSilva and my attack. I had certainly not forgotten any of this during the robbery ordeal. However, I would have to admit that the frenzy surrounding the apprehension of the individuals responsible for breaking into and robbing my home, gave me a chance to get as close to justice and a certain peace of mind as I had been able to do in months.

This was short-lived. I considered the day approaching when I would have the opportunity to face DeSilva in court. I would finally have my day in court to tell the story of how he had broken into my home and savagely beaten and tortured me. But, the potential gratification of telling my story and allowing the courts to seek justice for me is a double-edged sword. I want to let the world know how I have been driven to the brink of insanity and ridden an out of control roller coaster of emotions since this attack. I want people to know that this man not only attacked me physically, but he also stole my pride and my ability to ever feel safe again.

But, at the same time, by telling my story I am forced to relive it. By going back and recounting the details of that night of horror I am not sure of the toll it may take on me. Although I have certainly not forgotten what happened to me that night, I have not sat and dwelled on it. I will also be faced with seeing the evidence that was taken from my home by police.

Such as the blood-soaked blanket that I lay on as this man stabbed and beat me. This is the same blanket that my son and I had many times used to keep warm while we snuggled on the sofa to watch a movie together.

Seeking justice is not always a reward within itself. It is necessary, but does not come void of its own piece of misery. The more I am forced to think about the events of that night, the more I find the attack against me did not end as my assailant slammed the door leaving me for dead. It continues on and destroys parts of my life that are vital.

How could my son ever feel safe with me again. For over 10 years I had been mother and father, provider and protector. Within a few hours one night a complete stranger burst into my home and destroyed all I had felt was indestructible. All the precious memories that I had of my life in that home with my son were now tainted with the vile memories that were left me by this monster.

While I consider the relentless agony I endured at the hands of my attacker, I cannot help but only imagine what was happening to my child. Here was an 11-year-old boy who lay in a dark room by himself while his mother is beaten and stabbed just a few feet away. He was completely helpless to do anything without causing this man to carry out his threat to kill us both should Nathan wake up. No one, least of all a child, should be faced with an unfathomable dilemma like this. It breaks my heart that I was unable to be there for him at what I am sure was his darkest and most frightening moments.

I must find some way to deal with the reality of what has happened in my life and in my son's life. I must do this before I am led into a courtroom to face this monster and tell my story publicly. I must once again fall to my knees and seek the guidance and support of the only one who can truly understand my pain. I must turn to God to help me make this confusing and tumultuous journey toward victory.

A battered reed He will not break off, and a smoldering wick He will not put out, until He leads justice to victory.

Matthew 12:20

Chapter 11

The similarities were too close to dismiss. Was the man who tried to kill me also involved in the murder of a 17-year-old girl in Maryland? I was shocked to learn that while police in Delaware were investigating Douglas DeSilva in connection with my attack, police in northeast Maryland were also looking into him as well.

My heart sunk as I learned that DeSilva was a person of interest in the brutal murder of Julie Lynn Ferguson, a young girl from Greenbelt, Maryland, whose body was found lying on the side of a Glenn Dale, Maryland road. Like me, this young girl was beaten, stabbed and her throat cut.

According to police in Prince George's County, DeSilva, a mechanic, lived in Lanham, Maryland, only four miles from the shopping center where Julie Ferguson worked. Like so much trash, this beautiful, innocent girl was left lying along the side of the road until a motorist found her battered body at about 5:30 am., March 21, 1995.

My heart broke for her family. I took a personal interest in this case and learned that the girl had been working in a shopping center and called for a ride home at about 9:30 pm the previous night. Her ride arrived to pick her up at about 10 pm and found she was not there. Someone had seen her just 10 minutes earlier. All that was left behind was a bag containing some personal belongings.

Police said that DeSilva had been traveling back and forth from his home in nearby Lanham, Maryland, to Laurel several times a week. After he was arrested and charged in my attack, the similarities between my case and Julie Ferguson's murder led Delaware State Police and Prince George's County, Maryland police to begin sharing information. Police would not name DeSilva as a suspect, but simply "a person of interest."

The news caused me to realize just how lucky I was to survive my attack. I became even more determined to see this ordeal through to the end. I had to find justice somehow, no matter what it meant in terms of my own personal emotions.

There were times when I felt so emotionally drained and just wanted to give up and pretend to forget what had been done to me. But, learning about others, like the family of Julie Ferguson who must live with the horror and heartbreak of a brutal crime, made it even more clear to me that I had to do whatever I could to prevent another person from being hurt or killed.

With the Ferguson investigation in Maryland and my case working here in Delaware, it would only be a matter of time before DeSilva would be sitting in prison for the rest of his life. I knew it was an open and shut case. But, there was something I did not know; something that would suddenly bring my world down around me.

'Suspect in area woman's attack released'

As I read the headline in the local newspaper it was like salt being rubbed in a wound. After two years of waiting for my turn in the justice system, I had my day in court ripped out of my hands. To my utter disbelief, DeSilva was being released from prison and any further prosecution.

Friday, January 3, 1997, a day that I will most likely always consider the second worst day in my life. Just three days before the attempted murder trial against DeSilva was slated to start a judge slammed his gavel down and set him free; all 11 charges were dismissed. How could this be?

I had been notified a day earlier by Delaware Deputy Attorney General Jim Adkins, the chief prosecutor in the case that he was forced to dismiss charges against DeSilva. He told me that the evidence processed at FBI laboratories came back void of any DNA linking DeSilva to the crime. There was nothing to support his even being in my house that night at all. I was speechless and once again I was thrust headlong into a ball of confusion. I had identified this man as my attacker. My son had identified him as well. I spent hours being brutally assaulted by a man that the justice system was telling me was not DeSilva. I made it a point to be in the courtroom the next day, telling myself this was all a mistake and it would be corrected during the Friday afternoon court proceedings. I arrived at the Sussex County Superior Court building in Georgetown. This was only the second time since DeSilva was arrested in October, 1995, that I have been in a courtroom with him. Prior to this I attended his preliminary hearing.

I made sure to sit on the front row. I prayed to hear the judge say there had been a mistake and he would proceed with DeSilva's attempted murder trial. Those words never came. I watched as DeSilva was led to his seat, where he sat, arms folded, his eyes fixed on the Judge's bench.

I felt sick to my stomach. I felt like I would vomit at any moment. Within only five minutes, the judge announced that the state had dismissed charges against DeSilva and he was free to go. As the judge's gavel fell signaling the closing of the court proceedings, I could not find the strength to rise to my feet. I felt like I may faint.

As they led DeSilva out the back door of the courtroom, I made my way out of the courthouse, clinging to my mother's arm. On the steps of the courthouse reporters had gathered. I saw DeSilva's public defender, Stephen Callaway, being interviewed and could hear what he was saying.

"The state was correct to dismiss charges against my client," he told the reporters. "Mrs. Robinson gave four or five detailed statements to investigators as to what Mr. DeSilva was alleged to have done while at her home and the things he handled at the trailer, including the telephone, a Nintendo® game and a picture."

Callaway went on to explain why his client was now free to return home to his family in Maryland. "The Delaware State Police went through Mrs. Robinson's mobile home with the Crime Lab and found no fingerprints belonging to Mr. DeSilva on any of those items," he said.

"There was a shoe print found outside the trailer, but Mr. DeSilva owned no clothing that matched that shoe print or any of the clothing or jewelry that Mrs. Robinson said her attacker was wearing at the time of the incident," Callaway proclaimed.

I also learned that DeSilva's home and pickup truck were also analyzed and when blood samples were sent to the FBI for DNA testing, the FBI concluded that DeSilva was "absolutely not the person who left behind the DNA that was collected at the crime scene."

The final comments by Callaway were the most frustrating. "We have witnesses who were prepared to testify that Mr. DeSilva was in Maryland at the time of this attack," he claimed. "The state has been dealt a tremendous blow. All they have is Mrs. Robinson's identification. It's a real tragic situation. We have this woman who has been brutally assaulted and stabbed and the state has had the wrong guy locked up for it."

Over two years and we were now just learning that the only evidence the state had against DeSilva was my eye witness testimony? Why did it take the FBI so long to process evidence? Certainly mistakes could have been made in the handling of the evidence. I refused to believe that DeSilva was innocent. Yet, he was picked up following the court proceedings by his family and taken back home to Lanham, Maryland. In the courtroom during the final proceedings, Deputy Attorney General Jim Adkins told the presiding judge, Judge T. Henley Graves, that all evidence had not been fully processed by the FBI. He wanted the court to understand that should any evidence come back linking DeSilva to my crime, the state would bring charges against him and move forward with a trial.

These words were scarcely comforting. They rang hollow. There would be no evidence forthcoming from the FBI. DeSilva was free. He would not face prosecution. I would simply have to face the fact that I would not see my day in court - at least not against Douglas DeSilva.

He went home a victor, escaping the sword of justice. I went home feeling defeated. I had spent over two years awaiting the day when I would see correctional officers escorting DeSilva off to a prison cell where he would spend the remainder of his life. Instead he was escorted to a waiting vehicle and off to the comforts of his home.

The days passed and I became less and less satisfied with what had happened in the courtroom. A new found sense of despair overtook me. How could I have spent hours being tortured and brutally assaulted by a man and not remember what he looked like? As far as I was concerned the court system had released my attacker and renewed my fear of being once again attacked, or even killed.

The justice system had abandoned me. I felt truly alone in all of my misery. Because I had bought a gun and learned to use it, I was now contemplating the idea of bringing about my own justice. I was not about to be essentially called a liar and left to simply pick up the pieces and move on. I lay in bed night after night, playing out a plan in my mind to seek my own justice. I decided the time for thinking about it was over. If there was to be justice, I would need to take action.

I drove to Lanham, Maryland, found DeSilva's home and waited outside. I decided I would knock on his door and when he answered, ask if he remembered me. I would force him to look me in the eye and make sure I was the last thing he saw as I pulled the trigger on the gun and finally found justice.

I had finally reached my lowest point. I was now thinking like the man who had attacked me. I knew I was leaning completely on my own understanding and leaving God out. I began to pray and beg God to help me deal with the hurt and hate that seemed to ravage my entire being. I abandoned my plan and headed back to Delaware.

How could I be driven to the point where I felt it justified to execute my own vengeance and kill a man in order to find justice? How could I do something that after all was said and done, leave me in prison, separated from my son and all of my family?

I slowly began to accept that I may never feel a true sense of justice. There would be no closure in my case, at least not in the manner that I had envisioned. With God's help I would begin to try and put my life back together and play out the hand that I had been dealt.

I had responsibilities and a son to finish raising. It was time to move on and allow God to work in my life to find peace and the will to continue being the best mother I could be.

Did legal system fail to work?

Editorial from Laurel-Seaford Star newspaper,
Morning Star Publications, Inc., Seaford, Delaware
January, 1997

In America we have the greatest legal system in the world. However, sometimes that legal system is unable to produce the results that we may feel it should. On Friday, Jan. 3, in Superior Court, Georgetown, such a situation arose in which the legal system did not produce the results that some would have been hoping for.

As Brenda Kaye Robinson sat in the Courtroom, she watched and listened as the state of Delaware dismissed II charges, including kidnapping and attempted murder, against Douglas Leo DeSilva, rendering him a free man.

DeSilva had been held since September 1995, in the stabbing attack of Robinson in her Laurel-area home. He is the man that she had identified as her attacker. However, evidence gathered by the Delaware State Police and processed by the FBI did not support her claim. No one can pretend to understand the horror, the pain, the anger and now, the disappointment, that Robinson has endured over the past 18 months since her attack.

Those who know Kaye Robinson know her as a sweet, intelligent, truthful and courageous woman. However, the legal system that is dedicated to protecting our Constitutional rights was unable to produce the necessary physical evidence that would have been needed to support her claim and make a successful case against this defendant.

Though still a suspect, DeSilva has not been proven a criminal. Given the lack of physical evidence, the state was right in not moving forward with the case. Our Constitutional rights were not developed to benefit the criminal, as some people tend to believe. They were developed to protect the rights of those who are unjustly accused. Though our hearts bleed for Kaye Robinson, we must somehow still believe that our legal system is doing that which is necessary in regards to this case.

But, let us also not forget that the bottom line still remains. Someone brutally attacked Kaye Robinson. Her right to feel safe in her own home was savagely violated. While her son was sleeping in the next room a maniac spent hours butchering and torturing this innocent mother. Now, almost two years later, she has been denied the right to feel safe at any given time.

This recent legal setback must not spell an end to this case. It must instead revitalize the investigation efforts that we pray will lead to the arrest of the animal that is guilty of this heinous crime.

We cannot let this cause us to lose faith in the greatest legal system in the world. We pray, instead, that the state of Delaware will soon have the physical evidence it needs to fully prosecute the person who is responsible for stealing Kaye Robinson's ability to, ever feel truly safe again. This we feel is owed, not only to her, but to any others who have been or may be, the victims of this monster.

It is mine to avenge; I will repay. In due time their foot will slip; their day of disaster is near and their doom rushes upon them.
Deuteronomy 32: 35

Chapter 12

The days turned into weeks and weeks into months. After a decade I had transitioned out of being a crime victim, suffering through the mending of physical and emotional wounds. I was back to being an insurance agent, mother and now two-time grandmother. God is wonderful. Once I began to lean on Him and let go of so much of the pain that held me hostage, I truly began to heal. I accepted that the man I had identified as my attacker was not the perpetrator in the eyes of the judicial system. That was simply something I had

128

to deal with. I still had the looming doubts in my mind, but that is where they had to stay.

I was certainly not prepared for what was about to happen almost 10 years since the day of my attack. Detective Robert Hudson called me in October 2005, and told me there was a man serving a life sentence in Maryland for attempted murder. Delaware State Police believed this man to be my assailant.

Hudson told me that the man's name was Mark Eskridge and he was in prison for attacking a Dorchester County, Maryland, woman in 2002. He attacked the single mother in her mobile home in the same manner as I was assaulted in 1995.

As in my assault, police said once Eskridge accosted the woman in her bedroom, he tied her up, displayed a rolling pin and butcher knife and sexually assaulted her. However, unlike my experience, when the woman begged him not to hurt her son, Eskridge apologized and left the home, leaving the woman tied up but void of further physical harm. Hudson said in February 2005, Eskridge was on trial in

Dorchester County, Maryland for the attack that occurred in that state and a Laurel citizen attended the trial. The unidentified citizen lived in Laurel Village Mobile Home Park at the time of my assault. The citizen went to state police, noting the similarities of the two attacks, coupled with the fact that Mark Eskridge apparently also lived in Laurel Village Mobile Home Park at the time of my attack.

In March 2005, Delaware State Police were alerted that DNA they had acquired as evidence from my attack matched DNA samples taken from Eskridge. Police charged Eskridge with attempted first-degree murder, first-degree burglary, first-degree robbery, first-degree kidnapping, two counts of unlawful sexual contact in the first-degree and five counts of possession of a deadly weapon during the commission of a felony.

Mark Eskridge was being held on a half-million dollars bond in the same Sussex County, Delaware, correctional facility that DeSilva had stayed for two years. Once again a man was sitting behind bars accused of trying to kill me. This time DNA evidence supported the claim that Mark

Eskridge tried to kill me 10 years earlier. I was dumb-founded. I could not wrap my mind around this. I looked at the picture of Mark Eskridge and right away said this could not be the man who attacked me. He looks nothing like the man who spent four hours torturing me in my home.

Police brought a picture to me of Mark Eskridge as he looked in 1995. I was shocked. He could have been DeSilva's twin brother. The hair, the body size, everything was comparable. There is no question these two men fit the description of my attacker to a tee.

It was so hard to imagine that this man lived just a few homes away from me. All this time he had been walking around, living his life while mine was almost destroyed. Why did Douglas DeSilva thrust himself into my case and leave me and police convinced he was my attacker? This kept police focused on DeSilva while Mark Eskridge walked free and went on to attack at least one other woman.

The news of my case being solved brought me mixed emotions. Certainly I was happy that the man who had so brutally attacked me was now behind bars and I had a sense of closure. But, it forced me to once again relive the treacherous memories of the attack and the emotional roller coaster I had been on over the past 10 years.

Sadly, only a few days after learning of the arrest of Mark Eskridge, my faithful friend and companion for over a decade, "Cujo," died. The 125-pound Rottweiller dog was like a family member to me. She loved me and I loved her. She was always by my side, helping me to feel secure, even as time passed with no arrest in my case. It was as if once learning that the man who had hurt me was off the streets and unable to harm me, Cujo felt her job was done. She simply laid down and died.

In January 2006, Mark Eskridge pleaded guilty to my attack and was sentenced to life, plus 20 years. There is no way short of a Governor's Pardon that he can ever get out of prison. After 11 years and two arrests, justice was finally served.

Epilogue

I suppose there is no getting over the type of attack that I endured on that night in September 1995. There is no way to ever feel one hundred percent safe in my surroundings. However, the one thing that was constant for me; the one true guarantee that I had throughout my recovery was God's love. The grace of God's love surpasses my understanding and keeps me truly humble.

I know the fear of imminent death. I have felt the pain and depression that accompanies physical and emotional torment. I also know that daily so many people face these same feelings of despair as they meet and deal with any number of tragic circumstances.

I have not shared the details of my brutal, horrific attack as a means to exploit what are now tragic memories, and components of an event that should have left me dead, or at minimum, forever emotionally and physically scarred. I have always believed that we must find a silver lining in every storm cloud. There must be good found in every bad experience, a lesson learned. So, I want the "good" that has come about as the result of my brutal, hellish experience to be the message of hope that I accepted as I allowed God's healing love to transform me; transform me from a bitter, scarred, scared, insecure victim, into a productive, excited and appreciative victor!

Today, I am not only a single, working mother, but my son, Nathan, has now blessed me with two beautiful grandchildren. I live my life surrounded by the love of family and a stronger than ever determination to make sure that I view each day as a gift from God. As such, I feel so blessed with not only once again living an "ordinary life," but one that is enriched by the extraordinary love and grace of God.

Brenda Kaye Robinson